This Jo

The Daily Quote

The Daily Quote

Inspirations For A Calmer Mind

Created by

21 Exercises

Introduction

The Daily Quote is carefully created to inspire you on a daily basis. A moment of reflection, mindfulness and true motivation. We've chosen these 365 quotes because they hold meaning to us. Sentences from dazzling novels, poems of love and wisdom from all periods of mankind. Words calling to you from centuries ago, ancient China, ancient Rome. And quotes from the brightest minds of the 2000's. In our attempt to search for the more original quotes, we've searched through poems and literature as well as philosophical books.

Now, when our job is finished, we only hope that you may find your daily inspiration in these mysterious ocean of wisdom. We know that these quotes have the power to discover new opportunities, uncover insights about your own life and help you to find clarity & purpose. Within these 365 quotes words you will certainly find the words that speak specifically to you. The lessons you've learned, the insights you've gained or simply an everyday experience can be written down in the blank lines underneath the quote. It's an interactive book, and it's now up to you.

We hope you enjoy The Daily Quote, and that, with a calm and joyful heart, you may find what you're looking for!

DISCLAIMER
We tried our best to attribute each and every quote to the right person. We've respected the words as much as we could, and to our best knowledge we've stated the quote exactly as it was displayed in the work of the author. Therefore we also have maintained the original gender references. Nevertheless, each quote is equally applicable to all people.

How To Use *The Daily Quote*

Every page of this book contains three new days, posing a new, inspiring quote each day. Underneath the quote you'll find blank lines: the journaling space. First of all, the best way to use *The Daily Quote* is to do it on a daily basis, at the same time each day. For example during your morning routine or right before you go to bed. By choosing a particular time each day, you can easily integrate *The Daily Quote* as a short, simple habit in your life with remarkable positive effects.

Every seven days you'll find a short weekly reflection + a weekly journaling question.

The price of *The Daily Quote* is almost similar to the price of two Starbucks latte's. Not *Rockefeller* money. The question arises: what is the value of this book? Is a dollar a dollar? Well, the value is up to you. We've handpicked every quote in this journal carefully. Furthermore the weekly reflection + weekly journaling question are thoughtfully created to guide your journaling session. So the content we had to create is finished. If you just want to use *The Daily Quote* as a book, that's fine. It's going to be your companion whenever you need inspiration. The value of daily inspiration is priceless. So is the value of daily journaling. A day-to-day act of reflection. The print version of this book provides you with the space for writing. The space for daily reflection. However you want to use it, it's up to you.

Four journaling advices

- Use the quotes as writing exercise. Every day, for a couple of minutes, think about the meaning of the quote from that day. Then write down your thoughts. This daily exercise sharpens your thinking and will definitely lead to new ideas and new valuable insights.
- Use *The Daily Quote* as your everyday journal. Ideally for this, is to make it a habit just before you go to bed. In a couple of sentences write down what happened that day. You could use the quote from that day as inspiration. This way *The Daily Quote* becomes your autobiography for that year.

- Use *The Daily Quote* as your affirmation journal. For this journaling exercises it is best to do your writing each morning. Every day write down your affirmation for the coming day. You can use the quote from that day as inspiration.
- When you feel the need to contemplate life, open *The Daily Quote* on a random page. Read the quote and sit down with the words for three to five minutes. A short thoughtful meditation. Think about the meaning. How do these words reflect on your life? After your meditation write down your thoughts.

There are things known
and there are things unknown
and in between are the doors.

Jim Morrison

DAY 1

Forever is composed of nows.

Emily Dickinson

DAY 2

The last thing one discovers in composing a work is what to put first.

Blaise Pascal

DAY 3

It is therefore senseless to think of complaining since nothing foreign has decided what we feel, what we live, or what we are.

Jean-Paul Sartre

Day 4

Nothing that God ever made
is the same thing to more than one person.

Zora Neale Hurston

_____

_____

_____

_____

_____

_____

_____

_____

Day 5

Never close your lips to those
whom you have already opened your heart.

Charles Dickens

_____

_____

_____

_____

_____

_____

_____

_____

Day 6

Look back over the past, with its changing empires that rose and fell,
and you can foresee the future too.

Marcus Aurelius

_____

_____

_____

_____

_____

_____

_____

_____

Boredom: the desire for desires.

Leo Tolstoy

WEEKLY REFLECTION

Restriction leads to destruction. Why cage a bird?

What social conditions are preventing you from living the life that you want?

DAY 8

Every moment happens twice: inside and outside,
and they are two different histories.

Zadie Smith

DAY 9

Man is not worried by real problems so much
as by his imagined anxieties about real problems.

Epictetus

DAY 10

Love is heavy and light, bright and dark, hot and cold, sick and healthy,
asleep and awake- it's everything except what it is!

William Shakespeare

DAY 11

We accept the love we think we deserve.

Stephen chbosky

DAY 12

To do the useful thing, to say the courageous thing,
to contemplate the beautiful thing: that is enough for one man's life.

T.S. Eliot

DAY 13

Every life has death and every light has shadow.
Be content to stand in the light and let the shadow fall where it will.

Mary Stewart

Look within – there is no end!

Malebo Sephodi

WEEKLY REFLECTION

The depth of the human soul. The borders of the human mind.

What is your heart telling you to do?

DAY 15

If you don't know where you're going, any road'll take you there.

George Harrison

DAY 16

Sometimes you climb out of bed in the morning and you think, I'm not going to make it, but you laugh inside — remembering all the times you've felt that way.

Charles Bukowski

DAY 17

Love makes your soul crawl out from its hiding place.

Zora Neale Hurston

Day 18

No person has the right to rain on your dreams.

Marian Wright Edelman

Day 19

Destroy my desires, eradicate my ideals,
show me something better, and I will follow you.

Fyodor Dostoevsky

Day 20

I can't give you a sure-fire formula for success, but I can give you a
formula for failure: try to please everybody all the time.

Herbert Bayard Swope

It takes courage to grow up and become who you really are.

E.E. Cummings

WEEKLY REFLECTION

Oh, how sweet it is to stagnate...

Where in your life do you need more courage?

DAY 22

Whether you think you can, or you think you can't--you're right.

Henry Ford

DAY 23

The meeting of two personalities is like the contact of two chemical substances: if there is any reaction, both are transformed.

Carl Gustav Jung

DAY 24

Adventure is worthwhile in itself.

Amelia Earhart

DAY 25

Only someone who is well prepared has the opportunity to improvise.

Ingmar Bergman

DAY 26

If you judge people, you have no time to love them.

Mother Teresa

DAY 27

If a man will begin with certainties, he shall end in doubts; but if he will be content to begin with doubts, he shall end in certainties.

Francis Bacon

Believe nothing you hear, and only one half that you see.

Edgar Allan Poe

WEEKLY REFLECTION

Your perception makes your world.
Go beyond it and see the truth.

Try to look at your life from a distant. As an observer.
what do you see?

DAY 29

Love is that condition in which the happiness of another person is essential to your own.

Robert A. Heinlein

DAY 30

**To put everything in balance is good,
to put everything in harmony is better.**

Victor Hugo

DAY 31

One of the deep secrets of life is that all that is really worth the doing is what we do for others.

Lewis Carroll

DAY 32

We are what we pretend to be,
so we must be careful about what we pretend to be.

Kurt Vonnegut

DAY 33

I could not understand why men who knew all about good and evil
could hate and kill each other.

Mary Shelley

DAY 34

I have said it before, but I don't think I have ever came so near meaning
it.

Kate Chopin

I know who I am and who I may be, if I choose.

Miguel de cervantes Saavedra

WEEKLY REFLECTION

All around you, people with dreams, people with parents,
people with childhood.

How could you be more compassionate when judging other people?

DAY 36

I would always rather be happy than dignified.

Charlotte Brontë

DAY 37

The earth laughs in flowers.

Ralph Waldo Emerson

DAY 38

In the depth of winter, I finally learned that within me
there lay an invincible summer.

Albert Camus

DAY 39

Not all those who wander are lost.

J.R.R. Tolkien

DAY 40

It's a long old road, but I know I'm gonna find the end.

Bessie Smith

DAY 41

Anybody can sympathize with the sufferings of a friend,
but it requires a very fine nature to sympathize with a friend's success.

Oscar Wilde

**What do we live for,
if it is not to make life less difficult for each other?**

George Eliot

WEEKLY REFLECTION

**Is a setback really a setback, a mistake really a mistake?
Or is it merely a different kind of progress...**

What could you learn from a past mistake/setback?

DAY 43

I'm not in this world to live up to your expectations
and you're not in this world to live up to mine.

Bruce Lee

DAY 44

Music in the soul can be heard by the universe.

Lao Tzu

DAY 45

Words were different when they lived inside of you.

Benjamin Alire Sáenz

DAY 46

All my days I have longed equally to travel the right road
and to take my own errant path.

Sigrid Undset

DAY 47

When I look at my life and its secret colors,
I feel like bursting into tears.

Albert Camus

DAY 48

Attention is the rarest and purest form of generosity.

Simone Weil

Everybody gets so much information all day long
that they lose their common sense.

Gertrude Stein

_____

WEEKLY REFLECTION

Sometimes there are oceans between image and authentic self.

How is your image protecting you?

_____

The truth is rarely pure and never simple.

Oscar Wilde

You get what anybody gets - you get a lifetime.

Neil Gaiman

**It's really a wonder that I haven't dropped all my ideals, because they
seem so absurd and impossible to carry out.
Yet I keep them, because in spite of everything,
I still believe that people are really good at heart.**

Anne Frank

DAY 53

Fear is a disease that eats away at logic and makes man inhuman.

Marian Anderson

DAY 54

You talk when you cease to be at peace with your thoughts.

Kahlil Gibran

DAY 55

When there is no enemy within, the enemies outside cannot hurt you.

African Proverb

It's not the load that breaks you down, it's the way you carry it.

Lena Horne

WEEKLY REFLECTION

What a magnificent thing it is, to always have a choice.

How do you deal with taking responsibility?

DAY 57

The difference between genius and stupidity is: genius has its limits.

Alexandre Dumas

DAY 58

The role of a writer is not to say what we can all say,
but what we are unable to say.

Anaïs Nin

DAY 59

Life is long, if you know how to use it.

Lucius Annaeus Seneca

DAY 60

A concept is a brick. It can be used to build a courthouse of reason.
Or it can be thrown through the window.

Gilles Deleuze

DAY 61

I am not interested in being original. I am interested in being true.

Agostinho da Silva

DAY 62

Peace begins with a smile.

Mother Teresa

We may brave human laws, but we cannot resist natural ones.

Jules Verne

WEEKLY REFLECTION

The opposite of avoiding is embracing.

What are your mindful moments during the day?

Do what you can, with what you have, where you are.

Theodore Roosevelt

Wellbeing is the starting point not the end goal.

Frederick Dodson

Dreams are the touchstones of our characters.

Henry David Thoreau

DAY 67

It is nothing to die. It is frightful not to live.

Victor Hugo

DAY 68

Like all magnificent things, it's very simple.

Natalie Babbitt

DAY 69

**Great minds discuss ideas. Average minds discuss events.
Small minds discuss people.**

Henry Thomas Buckle

I have never met a man so ignorant
that I couldn't learn something from him.

Galileo Galilei

WEEKLY REFLECTION

What wisdom is all around you. The walking libraries called people.

What is the best advice you've received this year?

DAY 71

It's no use going back to yesterday,
because I was a different person then.

Lewis Carroll

DAY 72

You have everything needed
for the extravagant journey that is your life.

Carlos Castaneda

DAY 73

We have to dare to be ourselves, however frightening
or strange that self may prove to be.

May Sarton

DAY 74

To survive, you must tell stories.

Umberto Eco

DAY 75

The happiness of your life depends upon the quality of your thoughts.

Marcus Aurelius

DAY 76

Nothing contributes so much to tranquilize the mind
as a steady purpose.

Mary Shelley

If I am not good to myself,
how can I expect anyone else to be good to me?

Maya Angelou

WEEKLY REFLECTION

The one we spend the most time with throughout our lives...

How could you be a better friend to yourself?

DAY 78

The only true wisdom is in knowing you know nothing.

Socrates

DAY 79

Those who don't believe in magic will never find it.

Roald Dahl

DAY 80

Rain beats the leopards skin but it does not wash out the spots.

African proverb

DAY 81

Spring is the time of plans and projects.

Leo Tolstoy

DAY 82

Perhaps it is better to wake up after all, even to suffer, rather than to remain a dupe to illusions all one's life.

Kate Chopin

DAY 83

Man, when you lose your laugh you lose your footing.

Ken Kesey

The less people know, the more stubbornly they know it.

osho

WEEKLY REFLECTION

The more you know, the more you understand you know nothing.

what are the believes your life is built upon?

DAY 85

Learn to Walk Before You Run.

chinese proverb

_____

_____

_____

_____

_____

_____

_____

DAY 86

To die will be an awfully big adventure.

J.M. Barrie

_____

_____

_____

_____

_____

_____

_____

DAY 87

No one ever told me that grief felt so like fear.

c.S. Lewis

_____

_____

_____

_____

_____

_____

_____

Without music, life would be a mistake.

Friedrich Nietzsche

Never miss a good chance to shut up.

Will Rogers

If there's a book that you want to read,
but it hasn't been written yet, then you must write it.

Toni Morrison

Some people care too much. I think it's called love.

A.A. Milne

WEEKLY REFLECTION

Is it love, real love?

What is the difference between love and loyalty?

Most men would rather deny a hard truth than face it.

George R.R. Martin

If everybody minded their own business,
the world would go around a great deal faster than it does.

Lewis carroll

Facts are the enemy of truth.

Miguel de cervantes Saavedra

DAY 95

Sometimes, the best way to help someone is just to be near them.

Veronica Roth

DAY 96

The fool doth think he is wise,
but the wise man knows himself to be a fool.

William Shakespeare

DAY 97

When it is dark enough, you can see the stars.

Ralph Waldo Emerson

The best way out is always through.

Robert Frost

WEEKLY REFLECTION

Can you really think your way out of problems?

Where in your life are you focused too much on rationalizing?

DAY 99

Tis better to have loved and lost
Than never to have loved at all.

Alfred Lord Tennyson

DAY 100

You can't make decisions based on fear
and the possibility of what might happen

Michelle Obama

DAY 101

I love you as certain dark things are to be loved, in secret,
between the shadow and the soul.

Pablo Neruda

DAY 102

But the future must be met, however stern and iron it be.

Elizabeth Gaskell

DAY 103

Life is an awful, ugly place to not have a best friend.

Sarah Dessen

DAY 104

My religion is very simple. My religion is kindness.

Dalai Lama XIV

**The desire to reach for the stars is ambitious.
The desire to reach hearts is wise**

Maya Angelou

WEEKLY REFLECTION

The ego, hiding in a golden skyscraper.

what do you believe is your calling in life?

Happiness is when what you think, what you say,
and what you do are in harmony.

Mahatma Gandhi

How wonderful it is that nobody need wait a single moment
before starting to improve the world.

Anne Frank

I am not afraid of storms, for I am learning how to sail my ship.

Louisa May Alcott

DAY 109

Once you learn to read, you will be forever free.

Frederick Douglass

DAY 110

We are all in the gutter, but some of us are looking at the stars.

Oscar Wilde

DAY 111

Life is either a daring adventure or nothing at all.

Helen Keller

Day 112

Sarcasm is the last refuge of the imaginatively bankrupt.

cassandra clare

WEEKLY REFLECTION

How hard it is, to tell the truth.

What role does sarcasm play in your life?

DAY 113

Happiness always looks small while you hold it in your hands,
but let it go, and you learn at once how big and precious it is.

Maxim Gorky

DAY 114

Not everyone who chased the zebra caught it,
but he who caught it, chased it.

African proverb

DAY 115

There are more things in Heaven and Earth,
Horatio, than are dreamt of in your philosophy.

William Shakespeare

DAY 116

Life is a beautiful magnificent thing, even to a jellyfish.

Charles Chaplin

DAY 117

The cleverest of all, in my opinion,
is the man who calls himself a fool at least once a month.

Fyodor Dostoevsky

DAY 118

Be the change that you wish to see in the world.

Mahatma Gandhi

Happiness is something that comes into our lives
through doors we don't even remember leaving open.

Rose Wilder Lane

WEEKLY REFLECTION

Coincidence is the biggest secret in the universe...

What are your thoughts on luck / coincidence?

DAY 120

You're something between a dream and a miracle.

Elizabeth Barrett Browning

DAY 121

We must not wish for the disappearance of our troubles
but for the grace to transform them.

Simone Weil

DAY 122

The greatest weapon against stress
is our ability to choose one thought over another

William James

DAY 123

In order to be irreplaceable, one must always be different.

coco chanel

DAY 124

The world is a book and those who do not travel read only one page.

St. Augustine

DAY 125

Laughter is sunshine, it chases winter from the human face.

Victor Hugo

To love another person is to see the face of God.

Victor Hugo

_____

WEEKLY REFLECTION

Take a moment of gratitude
for all the people who make your life worthwhile.

How can you find balance between freedom and relationships?

_____

DAY 127

Whoever is careless with the truth in small matters cannot be trusted with important matters.

Albert Einstein

DAY 128

People tend to complicate their own lives, as if living weren't already complicated enough.

Carlos Ruiz Zafón

DAY 129

Never test the depth of water with both feet.

English proverb

DAY 130

Hope is a waking dream.

Aristotle

DAY 131

It's only after we've lost everything that we're free to do anything.

Chuck Palahniuk

DAY 132

Heard melodies are sweet, but those unheard, are sweeter.

John Keats

We are always the same age inside.

Gertrude Stein

WEEKLY REFLECTION

**What is the mind? What is the soul? What is the body?
Who are you?**

How old do you really feel?

DAY 134

Be kind, for everyone you meet is fighting a harder battle.

Plato

DAY 135

You never know what life is like, until you have lived it.

Marilyn Monroe

DAY 136

May you live every day of your life.

Jonathan Swift

DAY 137

Remember that very little is needed to make a happy life.

Marcus Aurelius

DAY 138

We dream in our waking moments, and walk in our sleep.

Nathaniel Hawthorne

DAY 139

One day I will find the right words, and they will be simple.

Jack Kerouac

I wish I could freeze this moment, right here,
right now and live in it forever.

Suzanne collins

WEEKLY REFLECTION

Some moments are so precious, they walk with you an entire lifetime.

How could you spend more time, money and effort on experiences?

It is better to offer no excuse than a bad one.

George Washington

Of all sad words of tongue or pen,
the saddest are these, 'It might have been.

John Greenleaf Whittier

Never be afraid to sit awhile and think.

Lorraine Hansberry

DAY 144

One must dare to be happy.

Gertrude Stein

DAY 145

The mind I love must have wild places.

Katherine Mansfield

DAY 146

None of us knows what might happen even the next minute,
yet still we go forward. Because we trust. Because we have Faith.

Paulo coelho

Freeing yourself was one thing,
claiming ownership of that freed self was another.

Toni Morrison

WEEKLY REFLECTION

Maybe the most difficult thing in the world
is to claim freedom with a sense of purpose.

What would you really do when you'd win 10 million dollars?
Would it make you happier?

DAY 148

Behind this mask there is more than just flesh.
Beneath this mask there is an idea... and ideas are bulletproof.

Alan Moore

DAY 149

Weak desire brings weak results,
just as a small fire makes a small amount of heat.

Napoleon Hill

DAY 150

I don't think there is any truth. There are only points of view.

Allen Ginsberg

DAY 151

Rain does not fall on one roof alone.

African proverb

DAY 152

Ask for what you want and be prepared to get it!

Maya Angelou

DAY 153

Those who cannot change their minds cannot change anything.

George Bernard Shaw

73

I want to stand as close to the edge as I can without going over. Out on the edge you see all kinds of things you can't see from the center.

Kurt Vonnegut

WEEKLY REFLECTION

Life is motion. Change is mandatory.

Where in your life do you need to change?

I am a part of all that I have met.

Alfred Tennyson

Self-esteem means knowing you are the dream.

Oprah Winfrey

Child, child, do you not see?
For each of us comes a time when we must be more than what we are.

Lloyd Alexander

DAY 158

My wish is that you may be loved to the point of madness.

André Breton

DAY 159

Life can only be understood backwards; but it must be lived forwards.

Søren Kierkegaard

DAY 160

Do what you feel in your heart to be right –
for you'll be criticized anyway.

Eleanor Roosevelt

Give light and people will find the way.

Ella Baker

WEEKLY REFLECTION

You attract what you are. And so you become.

If you were the average of your five closest friends/family members, who would you be?

DAY 162

Not knowing when the dawn will come
I open every door.

Emily Dickinson

DAY 163

You cannot protect yourself from sadness
without protecting yourself from happiness.

Jonathan Safran Foer

DAY 164

For you, a thousand times over.

Khaled Hosseini

We believe in ordinary acts of bravery,
in the courage that drives one person to stand up for another.

veronica Roth

It is the mark of an educated mind
to be able to entertain a thought without accepting it.

Aristotle

You only live once, but if you do it right, once is enough.

Mae West

Don't cry because it's over, smile because it happened.

Dr. Seuss

WEEKLY REFLECTION

Any experience could be for the last time.
This fundamental truth makes any experience even more remarkable.

How would this week be different if you'd fully grasp the inevitability of death?

DAY 169

And now here is my secret, a very simple secret: It is only with the heart that one can see rightly; what is essential is invisible to the eye.

Antoine de Saint-Exupéry

DAY 170

What draws people to be friends is that they see the same truth. They share it.

C. S. Lewis

DAY 171

We are all gifted. That is our inheritance.

Ethel Waters

DAY 172

Romance is the glamour which turns the dust of everyday life
into a golden haze.

Elinor Glyn

DAY 173

Each night, when I go to sleep, I die.
And the next morning, when I wake up, I am reborn.

Mahatma Gandhi

DAY 174

Keep your face always toward the sunshine –
and shadows will fall behind you.

Walt Whitman

Lock up your libraries if you like; but there is no gate, no lock, no bolt that you can set upon the freedom of my mind.

Virginia Woolf

WEEKLY REFLECTION

There is always freedom within you.

When do you feel other people restrict your freedom?

Day 176

Lovers don't finally meet somewhere. They're in each other all along.

Rumi

Day 177

The supreme art of war is to subdue the enemy without fighting.

Sun Tzu

Day 178

**I know nothing in the world that has as much power as a word.
Sometimes I write one, and I look at it, until it begins to shine.**

Emily Dickinson

Never be bullied into silence. Never allow yourself to be made a victim.
Accept no one's definition of your life; define yourself.

Robert Frost

If you want to know what a man's like,
take a good look at how he treats his inferiors, not his equals.

J.K. Rowling

I have spread my dreams under your feet.
Tread softly because you tread on my dreams.

W.B. Yeats

I have loved the stars too fondly to be fearful of the night.

Sarah Williams

WEEKLY REFLECTION

Darkness is only the absence of light.

what parts of your personality do you need to confront?

There is nothing either good or bad, but thinking makes it so.

William Shakespeare

DAY 184

A friend to all is a friend to none.

Aristotle

DAY 185

Everything we hear is an opinion, not a fact.
Everything we see is a perspective, not the truth.

Marcus Aurelius

DAY 186

Watch and pray, dear, never get tired of trying,
and never think it is impossible to conquer your fault.

Louisa May Alcott

DAY 187

He who knows all the answers has not been asked all the questions.

Confucius

DAY 188

Be steady and well-ordered in your life
so that you can be fierce and original in your work.

Gustave Flaubert

I wonder how many people I've looked at all my life and never seen.

John Steinbeck

_____

WEEKLY REFLECTION

If coincidence doesn't exist, everyone is a messenger.

**Reflect back on the past couple of months.
What is life trying to teach you?**

_____

Whatever you can do or dream you can, begin it.
Boldness has genius, power and magic in it!

John Anster

Laugh and the world laughs with you, snore and you sleep alone.

Anthony Burgess

That it will never come again is what makes life so sweet.

Emily Dickinson

DAY 193

We don't see things as they are, we see them as we are.

Anaïs Nin

DAY 194

I know not all that may be coming,
but be it what it will, I'll go to it laughing.

Herman Melville

DAY 195

There is nothing more deceptive than an obvious fact.

Arthur Conan Doyle

Human minds are more full of mysteries than any written book
and more changeable than the cloud shapes in the air.

Louisa May Alcott

WEEKLY REFLECTION

All that is has first existed in the human's imagination.

What dreams are frightening you?

DAY 197

The past beats inside me like a second heart.

John Banville

_____
_____
_____
_____
_____
_____
_____
_____

DAY 198

Someday you will be old enough to start reading fairy tales again.

C.S. Lewis

_____
_____
_____
_____
_____
_____

DAY 199

Hunger is the best sauce in the world.

Miguel de Cervantes Saavedra

_____
_____
_____
_____
_____
_____
_____

One must live as if it would be forever,
and as if one might die each moment. Always both at once.

Mary Renault

Dreams come true. Without that possibility,
nature would not incite us to have them.

John Updike

Love all, trust a few, do wrong to none.

William Shakespeare

Nature does not hurry, yet everything is accomplished.

Lao Tzu

WEEKLY REFLECTION

Who are we to argue with life?

Where in your life do you need to let go?

Procrastination is the thief of time, collar him.

Charles Dickens

_____

_____

_____

_____

_____

_____

_____

_____

_____

Love is so short, forgetting is so long.

Pablo Neruda

_____

_____

_____

_____

_____

_____

_____

_____

The wound is the place where the Light enters you.

Rumi

_____

_____

_____

_____

_____

_____

_____

_____

Day 207

To give pleasure to a single heart by a single act
is better than a thousand heads bowing in prayer.

Mahatma Gandhi

Day 208

The question is not what you look at, but what you see.

Henry David Thoreau

Day 209

Drop the idea of becoming someone, because you are already a
masterpiece. You cannot be improved.
You have only to come to it, to know it, to realize it.

Osho

Everyone on Earth, they'd tell us, was carrying around an unseen history,
and that alone deserved some tolerance.

Michelle Obama

WEEKLY REFLECTION

What would a little bit more compassion do
to the ocean of human emotion?

How could you be more compassionate to yourself?

Do you think that I count the days? There is only one day left, always starting over: it is given to us at dawn and taken away from us at dusk.

Jean-Paul Sartre

Nobody has ever measured, not even poets,
how much the heart can hold.

Zelda Fitzgerald

Be who you are and say what you feel, because those who mind don't matter, and those who matter don't mind.

Bernard M. Baruch

DAY 214

The impediment to action advances action.
What stands in the way becomes the way.

Marcus Aurelius

DAY 215

He felt that his whole life was some kind of dream and he sometimes
wondered whose it was and whether they were enjoying it.

Douglas Adams

DAY 216

Somewhere, something incredible is waiting to be known.

Carl Sagan

Our imagination flies — we are its shadow on the earth.

Vladimir Nabokov

WEEKLY REFLECTION

Where do thoughts come from?

How do you get inspired?

Day 218

In a time of deceit telling the truth is a revolutionary act.

George Orwell

Day 219

Nothing that's worthwhile is ever easy. Remember that.

Nicholas Sparks

Day 220

When one door of happiness closes, another opens;
but often we look so long at the closed door
that we do not see the one which has been opened for us.

Helen Keller

What a treacherous thing to believe that a person is more than a person.

John Green

If I had a flower for every time I thought of you...
I could walk through my garden forever.

Alfred Tennyson

Real generosity towards the future lies in giving all to the present.

Albert camus

Death is so terribly final, while life is full of possibilities.

George R.R. Martin

WEEKLY REFLECTION

Regret is such a loud alarm bell.

How could you be more spontaneous?

DAY 225

Men go to far greater lengths to avoid what they fear
than to obtain what they desire.

Dan Brown

DAY 226

I know you despise me; allow me to say,
it is because you do not understand me.

Elizabeth Gaskell

DAY 227

Others have seen what is and asked why.
I have seen what could be and asked why not.

Pablo Picasso

Do not spoil what you have by desiring what you have not; remember
that what you now have was once among the things you only hoped for.

Epicurus

You can't wait for inspiration. You have to go after it with a club.

Jack London

Only people who are capable of loving strongly can also suffer great
sorrow, but this same necessity of loving serves
to counteract their grief and heals them.

Leo Tolstoy

All good things are wild and free.

Henry David Thoreau

WEEKLY REFLECTION

Where goes all our potential?

**Do you live up to your potential?
Why or why not?**

DAY 232

Why fit in when you were born to stand out?

Dr. Seuss

DAY 233

When you have eliminated all which is impossible,
then whatever remains, however improbable, must be the truth.

Arthur Conan Doyle

DAY 234

We delight in the beauty of the butterfly, but rarely admit the changes
it has gone through to achieve that beauty.

Maya Angelou

DAY 235

Pain is inevitable. Suffering is optional.

Haruki Murakami

DAY 236

If you tell the truth, you don't have to remember anything.

Mark Twain

DAY 237

Our life is frittered away by detail.
Simplify, simplify.

Henry David Thoreau

If you can't explain it to a six year old, you don't understand it yourself.

Albert Einstein

_____

WEEKLY REFLECTION

We're using many and difficult words, just to bypass the truth.

How could you improve the relationship with yourself?

_____

Patience means knowing it will happen . . . and giving it time to happen.

Susan Jeffers

DAY 240

Life is a drama full of tragedy and comedy.
You should learn to enjoy the comic episodes a little more.

Jeannette Walls

DAY 241

All we have to decide is what to do with the time that is given us.

J.R.R. Tolkien

DAY 242

Throw your dreams into space like a kite, and you do not know what it will bring back, a new life, a new friend, a new love, a new country.

Anaïs Nin

DAY 243

Perhaps one did not want to be loved so much as to be understood.

George Orwell

DAY 244

Blessed are the hearts that can bend; they shall never be broken.

Albert Camus

Every heart sings a song, incomplete, until another heart whispers back.
Those who wish to sing always find a song.
At the touch of a lover, everyone becomes a poet.

Plato

WEEKLY REFLECTION

And the mind sweeps off the dance flour.

Try to describe the 'music' in your life.

Educating the mind without educating the heart is no education at all.

Aristotle

He who does not know one thing knows another.

African proverb

I've learned that people will forget what you said, people will forget what you did, but people will never forget how you made them feel.

Maya Angelou

DAY 249

Darkness cannot drive out darkness: only light can do that.
Hate cannot drive out hate: only love can do that.

Martin Luther King Jr.

DAY 250

Music is ... A higher revelation than all Wisdom & Philosophy.

Ludwig van Beethoven

DAY 251

The soul becomes dyed with the colour of its thoughts.

Marcus Aurelius

You can only be jealous of someone
who has something you think you ought to have yourself.

Margaret Atwood

WEEKLY REFLECTION

Jealousy cages your energy.

How would you describe jealousy?

Day 253

You can't stay in your corner of the Forest
waiting for others to come to you. You have to go to them sometimes.

A.A. Milne

Day 254

To understand the limitation of things, desire them.

Lao Tzu

Day 255

We are like islands in the sea,
separate on the surface but connected in the deep.

William James

Being busy is a form of laziness - lazy thinking and indiscriminate action.

Tim Ferriss

The 5 Second Rule The moment you have an instinct to act on a goal you must 5-4-3-2-1 and physically move or your brain will stop you.

Mel Robbins

All cruelty springs from weakness.

Seneca

One ought, every day at least, to hear a little song, read a good poem,
see a fine picture, and, if it were possible,
to speak a few reasonable words.

Johann Wolfgang von Goethe

WEEKLY REFLECTION

Oh precious time, be my lover, be my friend.
Be my night, be my day.

Describe your perfect day.

DAY 260

Get busy living or get busy dying.

Stephen King

DAY 261

Things change. And friends leave. Life doesn't stop for anybody.

Stephen chbosky

DAY 262

What is that you express in your eyes?
It seems to me more than all the print I have read in my life.

walt whitman

DAY 263

A great many people think they are thinking
when they are merely rearranging their prejudices.

William James

DAY 264

Until I feared I would lose it, I never loved to read.
One does not love breathing.

Harper Lee

DAY 265

Let our scars fall in love.

Galway Kinnell

I shut my eyes and all the world drops dead;
I lift my eyes and all is born again.

Sylvia Plath

WEEKLY REFLECTION

Close your eyes and see the sky of the mind.

When did you feel totally at peace?

DAY 267

Only those who will risk going too far
can possibly find out how far one can go.

T.S. Eliot

DAY 268

Of ignorant people
I am accustomed to consider the mere scientist the most ignorant!

M.P. Shiel

DAY 269

I like this place and could willingly waste my time in it.

William Shakespeare

...and then, I have nature and art and poetry,
and if that is not enough, what is enough?

Vincent van Gogh

If you have the words,
there's always a chance that you'll find the way.

Seamus Heaney

I have drunken deep of joy, And I will taste no other wine tonight.

Percy Bysshe Shelley

I have learned not to worry about love;
but to honor its coming with all my heart.

Alice Walker

WEEKLY REFLECTION

Love is killed by expectancy.

What is your greatest worry when it comes to love?

My turn shall also come: I sense the spreading of a wing.

Osip Mandelstam

It is not the man who has too little,
but the man who craves more, that is poor.

Seneca

Lovers alone wear sunlight.

E.E. cummings

DAY 277

Perhaps the truth depends on a walk around the lake.

Wallace Stevens

DAY 278

I wasn't actually in love, but I felt a sort of tender curiosity.

F. Scott Fitzgerald

DAY 279

I sing the song of my heartstrings,
alone in the eternal muteness, in the face of God.

Yone Noguchi

Those who are willing to be vulnerable move among mysteries.

Theodore Roethke

WEEKLY REFLECTION

Vulnerability is the biggest strength.

What are your thoughts on vulnerability?

DAY 281

Now that she had nothing to lose, she was free.

Paulo coelho

DAY 282

How wonderful it is that nobody need wait a single moment
before starting to improve the world.

Anne Frank

DAY 283

There is never a time or place for true love. It happens accidentally,
in a heartbeat, in a single flashing, throbbing moment

Sarah Dessen

DAY 284

The willing are led by fate, the reluctant are dragged.

cleanthes

DAY 285

**Given the choice between the experience of pain and nothing,
I would choose pain.**

William Faulkner

DAY 286

Is it really possible to tell someone else what one feels?

Leo Tolstoy

That is what learning is. You suddenly understand something you've understood all your life, but in a new way.

Doris Lessing

_____

WEEKLY REFLECTION

The knowledge is already within.

What is your favorite strategy for learning?

_____

DAY 288

Your conscience troubles you unnecessarily,
and you see a deliberate intention in every simple act.

Emma Orczy

DAY 289

Peace is always beautiful.

Walt Whitman

DAY 290

Into the darkness they go, the wise and the lovely.

Edna St. Vincent Millay

And the day came when the risk to remain tight in a bud
was more painful than the risk it took to blossom.

Anaïs Nin

DAY 292

Beauty is eternity gazing at itself in a mirror.
But you are eternity and you are the mirror.

Kahlil Gibran

DAY 293

Rather than love, than money, than fame, give me truth.

Henry David Thoreau

It is strange how often a heart must be broken
Before the years can make it wise.

Sara Teasdale

WEEKLY REFLECTION

If wisdom is already within, why does it come with age...

what are your three biggest lessons from last year?

For myself I would desire a combination of old romance
and modern machinery.

Flora Thompson

Life is essentially an endless series of problems.
The solution to one problem is merely the creation of another.

Mark Manson

What is this life so full of care,
We don't have time to stand and stare.

William Henry Davies

DAY 298

Traditions and customs which had lasted for centuries
did not die out in a moment.

Flora Thompson

DAY 299

In the prison of his days
Teach the free man how to praise.

W.H. Auden

DAY 300

I have a huge and savage conscience
that won't let me get away with things.

Octavia E. Butler

It requires a very unusual mind
to undertake the analysis of the obvious.

Alfred North Whitehead

_____
_____
_____
_____
_____
_____
_____
_____

WEEKLY REFLECTION

Is there a center in between all the 'you's'?

What are your obstacles when it comes to self-reflection?

_____
_____
_____
_____
_____
_____
_____
_____
_____
_____
_____
_____
_____
_____
_____
_____

DAY 302

Surely we should all perish through sheer inanity,
or die desperately by suicide if no mystery remained in the world.

J. D. Beresford

DAY 303

Vulnerability is the birthplace of innovation, creativity and change.

Brene Brown

DAY 304

You can't build a reputation on what you are going to do.

Henry Ford

DAY 305

I do not even deserve praise for doing my best, for that is my duty
and I deserve to be blamed for not doing my best.

Wanda Gág

DAY 306

As much as I live I shall not imitate them
or hate myself for being different to them.

Orhan Pamuk

DAY 307

Civilization advances by extending the number of important operations
which we can perform without thinking of them.

Alfred North Whitehead

What matters in life is not what happens to you
but what you remember and how you remember it.

Gabriel Garcia Marquez

WEEKLY REFLECTION

The accuracy of our memories: fading dreams.

**Write down your three best memories.
Just pick the first three that come to mind.**

We all have our time machines, don't we. Those that take us back are memories...And those that carry us forward, are dreams.

H.G. Wells

It was a scary thought.
A man could be surrounded by poetry reading and not know it.

Richard Russo

Receive with simplicity everything that happens to you.

Rashi

DAY 312

The course of true love never did run smooth.

William Shakespeare

DAY 313

What drains your spirit drains your body.
What fuels your spirit fuels your body.

carolyn Myss

DAY 314

Receive without conceit, release without struggle.

Marcus Aurelius

The art of progress is to reserve order amid change,
and to preserve change amid order.

Alfred North Whitehead

WEEKLY REFLECTION

It takes courage to see the beauty of life.

In what area of your life do you often complain?

What lies behind us and what lies before us
are tiny matters compared to what lies within us.

Ralph Waldo Emerson

When my information changes, I alter my conclusions.

John Maynard Keynes

Words are but the vague shadows of the volumes we mean. Little audible
links, they are, chaining together great inaudible feelings and purposes.

Theodore Dreiser

DAY 319

Morning without you is a dwindled dawn.

Emily Dickinson

DAY 320

**The power of finding beauty in the humblest things
makes home happy and life lovely.**

Louisa May Alcott

DAY 321

**We are like chameleons, we take our hue
and the color of our moral character, from those who are around us.**

John Locke

It is our collective and individual responsibility to preserve and tend to the environment in which we all live.

Dalai Lama

WEEKLY REFLECTION

Nature isn't endangered, it's us.

What is your responsibility when it comes to preservering and tending to the environment in which we all live?

DAY 323

My wealth is in my knowledge of self, love, and spirituality.

Muhammad Ali

DAY 324

It is a narrow mind
which cannot look at a subject from various points of view.

George Eliot

DAY 325

To be wronged is nothing, unless you continue to remember it.

Confucius

DAY 326

Bitterness is the coward's revenge on the world for having been hurt.

Zora Neale Hurston

DAY 327

The sea is not less beautiful in our eyes
because we know that sometimes ships are wrecked by it.

Simone Weil

DAY 328

Who you are is defined by what you're willing to struggle for.

Mark Manson

Don't let a day go by without asking who you are...
each time you let a new ingredient to enter your awareness.

Deepak chopra

WEEKLY REFLECTION

Better questions lead to better answers.

What did you learn this week?

Without deviation from the norm, progress is not possible.

Frank Zappa

Perfumes are the feelings of flowers.

Heinrich Heine

Do not fear to be eccentric in opinion,
for every opinion now accepted was once eccentric.

Bertrand Russell

DAY 333

The only defense against the world is a thorough knowledge of it.

John Locke

DAY 334

Ah! There is nothing like staying at home, for real comfort.

Jane Austen

DAY 335

Doing nothing is better than being busy doing nothing.

Lao Tzu

It is at the edge of the petal
that love waits

William carlos williams

WEEKLY REFLECTION

Even if love knocks on the door, you have to open it.

How is your mind interfering your love life?

DAY 337

How can you waste time?
You have only so much to use, and no matter what you do, it still passes.

Felix Salten

DAY 338

You attract what you need like a lover.

Gertrude Stein

DAY 339

Every new beginning comes from some other beginning's end.

Lucius Annaeus Seneca

I think I am, therefore, I am... I think.

George Carlin

Each of us narrates our life as it suits us.

Elena Ferrante

Even the finest sword plunged into salt water will eventually rust.

Sun Tzu

Truth is not a path you follow,
but one created by your footsteps.

Frederick E. Dodson

WEEKLY REFLECTION

What is the dream, what is the truth?

What exactly do you seek from others?

DAY 344

The whole banquet is in the first spoonful.

Deepak Chopra

DAY 345

All I know is a door into the dark

Seamus Heaney

DAY 346

One must wait until the evening to see how splendid the day has been.

Sophocles

DAY 347

Life changes in the instant. The ordinary instant.

Joan Didion

DAY 348

What loneliness is more lonely than distrust?

George Eliot

DAY 349

And while there is life
there is always the chance that something might happen...

Antal Szerb

Love is the only thing you can really give in all this world.
When you give love, you give everything.

Theodore Dreiser

WEEKLY REFLECTION

The mind is our addiction.

To what thoughts are you addicted?

DAY 351

It is never too late to be what you might have been.

George Eliot

DAY 352

But luxury has never appealed to me, I like simple things, books, being alone, or with somebody who understands.

Daphne du Maurier

DAY 353

Your task is not to seek for love, but merely to seek and find all the barriers within yourself that you have built against it.

Rumi

DAY 354

Challenges are gifts that force us to search for a new center of gravity.
Don't fight them. Just find a new way to stand.

Oprah Winfrey

DAY 355

We belong far less to where we've come from
\than where we want to go.

Franz Werfel

DAY 356

If anyone on the verge of action should judge himself according to the
outcome, he would never begin.

Søren Kierkegaard

Fault always lies in the same place: with him weak enough to lay blame.

Stephen King

WEEKLY REFLECTION

Responsibility releases the burden.

If you would die today, what would you regret not doing?
And not seeing?
And not saying?

I like this place and could willingly waste my time in it.

William Shakespeare

Nature is pleased with simplicity. And nature is no dummy.

Isaac Newton

Nothing happens to anybody which he is not fitted by nature to bear.

Marcus Aurelius

DAY 361

Life is what happens to us while we are making other plans.

Allen Saunders

DAY 362

Imagination does not become great until human beings,
given the courage and the strength, use it to create.

Maria Montessori

DAY 363

You will never be happy if you continue to search for what happiness
consists of. You will never live if you are looking for the meaning of life.

Albert Camus

There are moments when we resort to senseless formulations and advance absurd claims to hide straightforward feelings.

Elena Ferrante

WEEKLY REFLECTION

Words orchestrating a wall of sound to hide the feelings.

What feelings are you hiding behind a wall of thoughts and words?

I don't know half of you half as well as I should like;
and I like less than half of you half as well as you deserve.

J.R.R. Tolkien

YEARLY REFLECTION

What a pleasure it is, the simple art of kindness.

write a letter to yourself, to be opened one year from now.

About The Authors

We specialize in creating empowering, elegant & inspirational self-help journals. The power of journaling, of consistent self-reflection, is a scientifically proven habit that will benefit your life in truly astonishing ways. Mainly 90-Day or Yearly Journals, on various topics and for all types of people. Tools for self-reflection, gratitude & personal growth.

We create each journal or workbook with the utmost care and the honest intention to give lasting benefit to our customers. We hope to guide you through releasing limitations and discover your hidden potentials in all areas of life. And of course to give an enjoyable journaling experience.

Step by step, to unlock the true you. Step by step, to a better world. We'd love to hear your ideas, tips, and questions. Let us know at exercises21@yahoo.com

The Daily Quote

Manufactured by Amazon.ca
Bolton, ON